Lean And Green Cookbook

The Best Beginner's Guide To Simple And Healthy Recipes To Help You Burn Fat And Lose Weight. Recipes From Breakfast to Dinner

Do you want to take a look at our recipes?

Then just turn on your phone's camera, and you'll be automatically head over to our official Instagram page and follow us!

TASTEACADEMYBOOK

TABLE OF CONTENTS

.

Introduction

My story begins seven years ago at almost 60 lbs. I was on a mission to transform my body into something healthier. I was introduced to many new diets and exercise programs, some of which failed to achieve any significant results, and others made a small contribution to my weight loss. The internet is full of amazing diets that promise to help me lose a lot of weight with little effort, but fail to deliver. Nothing came close to achieving my weight loss goal. Then I discovered the Lean and Green diet. I was thrilled with the supplies I received for the plan I chose, but the Lean and Green meals are proving to be a tough nut to crack because I don't know what to prepare that meets the diet's recommendations.

I wish I could take the guesswork out of the whole process to focus on taking the portions of food provided and not spend too much time following the nutritional information. However, with the guidance of my dietitian, I was able to combine some vegetable recipes to make a healthy diet. Despite this, the process was nerve-wracking. I documented the recipes and diets, followed the diet strictly and experienced excellent results. I lost weight beyond my expectations and developed a new relationship with food. Six years later, I am still active, strong and maintaining a healthy weight. Eating Lean & Green has become part of my lifestyle, and I have documented my Lean and Green diet in this cookbook to help you make a healthy choice with your diet .
I have struggled with an unhealthy body weight for most of my life, the inspiration to write this diet book comes from a deep desire to help others on a similar journey. I'm excited to share nutritious and healthy Lean and Green diets that are also incredibly satisfying and delicious.As you know, the Lean and Green diet is a commercial diet, but it is considered one of the most popular diets that have brought many

benefits over the three decades. Lean and Green is a home cooked meal option that encourages weight loss through strict homemade green recipes to improve blood lipids, sugar levels and better overall health. Lean and Green is an easy, affordable, and long-lasting diet to lose weight quickly and effectively. This book will be your guide so that you can enjoy delicious and healthy food that can improve your health.

Are you tired of diets that promise results but take a huge amount of time and effort to plan? Or are you looking for a diet that will help you lose unnecessary weight in a fast, safe and convenient way? You can finally stop agonizing over losing time, money or inspiration with this Lean and Green cookbook. The recipes in this book will help you lose weight in the shortest possible time, and will also boost your confidence and promote motivation to continue.

The recipes contain ingredients that will help you lose weight and maintain good overall health without worrying about regaining the weight in the future.
This book helps you develop a healthy relationship with food while educating you with the health benefits and nutritional information in each of the recipes.
Soon, preparing a healthy diet will be a breeze, as you now have the information on how to prepare meals that fit your needs.

CHAPTER 1

BREAKFAST RECIPES

1. Prickly Pear Juice

Prep Time: 5 mins

Cook Time: 10 mins

Servings: 2

Ingredients:

- 6 Prickly Pears   1/3 cup of Lime Juice

- 1/3 cup of Agave   1/2 cups of Spring Water

Directions:

1. Take Prickly Pear, cut off the ends, slice off the skin, and put in a blender. Do the same with the other pears.

2. Add Lime Juice with Agave to the blender and blend well for 30–40 seconds.

3. Strain the prepared mixture through a nut milk bag or cheesecloth and pour it back into the blender.

4. Pour Spring Water in and blend it repeatedly.

5. Serve and enjoy your Prickly Pear Juice!

6. *Tips*: If you want a cold drink, add ice cubes.

Nutrition:

- Calories: 312

- Fat: 6g

- Carbs: 11g

- Protein: 8g

- Fiber: 2g

2. Soursop Smoothie

Prep Time: 5 mins

Cook Time: 5 mins

Servings: 2

Ingredients:

- 3 quartered frozen Burro Bananas

- 1/2 cups of Homemade Coconut Milk

- 1/4 cup of Walnuts

- 1 teaspoon of Sea Moss Gel   1 teaspoon of Ground Ginger   1

  teaspoon of Soursop Leaf Powder

- 1 handful of Kale

Directions:

1. Prepare and put all ingredients in a blender or a food
   processor.

2. Blend it well until you reach a smooth consistency.

3. Serve and enjoy your Soursop Smoothie!

4. *Tips*: If you don't have frozen Bananas, you can use fresh
   ones.

Nutrition:

- Calories: 213

- Fat: 3.1g

- Carbs: 6g

- Protein: 8g

- Fiber: 4.3g

3. <u>Sausage Ricotta Cheese Casserole</u>

Prep Time: 5 mins

Cook Time: 30 mins

Servings: 6

<u>Ingredients</u>:

- 5 eggs

- 1 1/2 lbs Italian sausage

- 1 tbsp fresh basil, chopped

- 6 cherry tomatoes, halved

- 8 oz ricotta cheese, cut into cubes

- 2 oz cream cheese

- 1 tsp salt

<u>Directions</u>:

1. Preheat the oven to 400 F.

2. Add sausage into the casserole dish and bake for 20 minutes. Once done, drain sausage well and break in small pieces using a masher.

3. In a bowl, whisk eggs with cream cheese until smooth and pour over sausage. Season with salt. Sprinkle ricotta cheese cubes, tomatoes, and basil on top.

4. Bake for 35-40 minutes more.

Nutrition:

- Calories: 240

- Fat: 18 g

- Carbohydrates: 4 g

- Sugar 1.7 g

- Protein 16 g

4. <u>Egg & Bacon Cups</u>

Prep Time: 10 mins

Cook Time: 15 mins

Servings: 4

<u>Ingredients</u>:

- 2 bacon strips

- 2 large eggs

- Handful of fresh spinach

- ¼ cup cheese

- Salt and pepper to taste

<u>Directions</u>:

1. Preheat your oven to 400 degrees Fahrenheit.

2. Fry bacon in a skillet over medium heat, drain the oil and keep them on the side.

3. Take muffin tin and grease with oil.

4. Line with a slice of bacon, press down the bacon well, making sure that the ends are sticking out (to be used as handles).

5. Take a bowl and beat eggs.

6. Drain and pat the spinach dry.

7. Add the spinach to the eggs.

8. Add a quarter of the mixture in each of your muffin tins.

9. Sprinkle cheese and season.

10. Bake for 15 minutes.

Nutrition:

- Calories: 101

- Fat: 7 g

- Carbohydrates: 2 g

- Protein: 8 g

5. Coconut Porridge

Prep Time: 15 mins

Cook Time: 0 mins

Servings: 2

Ingredients:

- 2 tablespoons coconut flour

- 2 tablespoons vanilla protein powder

- 3 tablespoons Golden Flaxseed Meal

- 1½ cups almond milk, unsweetened

- Powdered Erythritol

Directions:

1. Take a bowl, mix in flaxseed meal, protein powder, coconut

   flour, and mix well.

2. Add mix to a saucepan (placed over medium heat).

3. Add almond milk and stir, let the mixture thicken.

4. Add your desired amount of sweetener and serve. Enjoy!

Nutrition:

- kcal: 236 g

- Carbohydrates: 6 g

- Protein: 18 g

- Fat: 12 g

6. Avocado Chicken Salad

Prep Time: 5 mins

Cook Time: 10 mins

Servings: 2

Ingredients:

- 10 oz diced cooked chicken

- ½ cup 2% Plain Greek yogurt

- 3 oz chopped avocado 12 tsp garlic powder

- ¼ tsp salt   1/8 tsp pepper

- 1 tbsp + 1 tsp lime juice

- ¼ cup fresh cilantro, chopped

Directions:

1. Combine all ingredients in a medium-sized bowl. Refrigerate

   until ready to serve.

2. Cut the chicken salad in half and serve with your favorite

greens.

Nutrition:

- kcal: 193 g

- Carbohydrates: 4 g

- Protein: 37 g

- Fat: 12 g

7. Banana Barley Porridge

Prep Time: 15 mins

Cook Time: 5 mins

Servings: 2

Ingredients:

- 1 cup divided unsweetened coconut milk

- 1 small peeled and sliced banana

- 1/2 cup barley

- 3 drops liquid stevia

- 1/4 cup chopped coconuts

Directions:

1. In a bowl, properly mix barley with half of the coconut milk

   and stevia.

2. Cover the mixing bowl then refrigerate for about 6 hours.

3. In a saucepan, mix the barley mixture with coconut milk.

4. Cook for about 5 minutes on moderate heat.

5. Then top it with the chopped coconuts and the banana slices.

6. Serve.

Nutrition:

- kcal: 158 g

- Carbohydrates: 19.5 g

- Protein: 4.7 g

- Fat: 7.4 g

8. Whole grain bread and avocado

Prep Time: 5 mins

Cook Time: 0 mins

Servings: 1

Ingredients:

- 2 slices of whole meal bread

- 60 g of cottage cheese

- 1 stick of thyme

- ½ avocado

- ½ lime

- Chili flakes

- salt pepper

Directions:

1. Cut the avocado in half.

2. Remove the pulp and cut it into slices.

3. Pour the lime juice over it.

4. Wash the thyme and shake it dry.

5. Remove the leaves from the stem.

6. Brush the whole wheat bread with the cottage cheese.

7. Place the avocado slices on top.

8. Top with the chili flakes and thyme.

9. Add salt and pepper and serve.

Nutrition:

- kcal: 462 g

- Carbohydrates: 26 g

- Protein: 22 g

- Fat: 17 g

9. Coconut Pancakes

Prep Time: 5 mins

Cook Time: 15 mins

Servings: 4

Ingredients:

- 1 cup coconut flour

- 2 tbsps. arrowroot powder

- 1 tsp. baking powder

- 1 cup coconut milk

- 3 tbsps. coconut oil

Directions:

1. In a medium container, mix in all the dry ingredients.

2. Add the coconut milk and 2 tbsps. of the coconut oil then mix properly.

3. In a skillet, melt 1 tsp. of coconut oil.

4. Pour a ladle of the batter into the skillet then swirl the pan to spread the batter evenly into a smooth pancake.

5. Cook it for like 3 minutes on medium heat until it becomes firm.

6. Turn the pancake to the other side then cook it for another 2 minutes until it turns golden brown.

7. Cook the remaining pancakes in the same process.

8. Serve.

Nutrition:

- kcal: 367 g

- Carbohydrates: 50.2 g

- Protein: 6.3 g

- Fat: 14.6 g

CHAPTER 2

LUNCH RECIPES

10. Bacon Wrapped Asparagus

Prep Time: 15 mins

Cook Time: 20 mins

Servings: 2

Ingredients:

- 1/3 cup heavy whipping cream

- 2 bacon slices, precooked

- 4 small spears asparagus

- Salt, to taste

- 1 tablespoon butter

Directions:

1. Preheat the oven to 360 degrees and grease a baking sheet with butter. Meanwhile, mix cream, asparagus and salt in a bowl. Wrap the asparagus in bacon slices and arrange them in the baking dish.

2. Transfer the baking dish to the oven and bake for about 20 minutes. Remove from the oven and serve hot.

3. Place the bacon wrapped asparagus in a dish and set aside to cool for meal prepping. Divide it in 2 containers and cover the lid. Refrigerate for about 2 days and reheat in the microwave before serving.

Nutrition:

- Calories: 204 kcal Fat: 20 g Carbs: 1.4 g Protein: 6.0 g

11. <u>Lemongrass Prawns</u>

Prep Time: 10 mins

Cook Time: 15 mins

Servings: 2

<u>Ingredients</u>:

- ½ red chili pepper, seeded and chopped

- 2 lemongrass stalks

- ½ pound prawns, deveined and peeled

- 6 tablespoons butter

- ¼ teaspoon smoked paprika

<u>Directions</u>:

1. Preheat the oven to 390 degrees and grease a baking dish.

2. Mix together red chili pepper, butter, smoked paprika and prawns in a bowl.

3. Marinate for about 2 hours and then thread the prawns on the lemongrass stalks.

4. Arrange the threaded prawns on the baking dish and transfer it in the oven.

5. Bake for about 15 minutes and dish out to serve immediately.

6. Place the prawns in a dish and set aside to cool for meal prepping. Divide it in 2 containers and close the lid. Refrigerate for about 4 days and reheat in microwave before serving.

Nutrition: Calories: 322 kcal ; Fat: 18 g ; Carbs: 3.8 g ; Protein: 34.8

12. Zucchini Pizza

Prep Time: 10 mins

Cook Time: 15 mins

Servings: 2

Ingredients:

- 1/8 cup spaghetti sauce

- ½ zucchini, cut in circular slices

- ½ cup cream cheese   Pepperoni slices, for topping   ½ cup mozzarella cheese, shredded

Directions:

1. Preheat the oven to 350 degrees and grease a baking dish.

2. Arrange the zucchini on the baking dish and layer with spaghetti sauce.

3. Top with pepperoni slices and mozzarella cheese.

4. Transfer the baking dish to the oven and bake for about 15

   minutes.

5. Remove from the oven and serve immediately.

Nutrition:

- Calories: 445 kcal

- Fat: 42 g

- Carbs: 3.6 g

- Protein: 12.8

13. Salmon Burgers

Prep Time: 10 mins

Cook Time: 15 mins

Servings: 4

Ingredients:

- 1 lb. salmon fillets

- 1 onion

- ¼ dill fronds

- 1 tablespoon honey

- 1 tablespoon horseradish

- 1 tablespoon mustard

- 1 tablespoon olive oil

- 2 toasted split rolls

- 1 avocado

Directions:

1. Place salmon fillets in a blender and blend until smooth, transfer to a bowl, add onion, dill, honey, horseradish and mix well

2. Add salt and pepper and form 4 patties

3. In a bowl combine mustard, honey, mayonnaise and dill   In a skillet heat oil add salmon patties and cook for 2-3 minutes per side

4. When ready remove from heat

5. Divided lettuce and onion between the buns

6. Place salmon patty on top and spoon mustard mixture and avocado slices   Serve when ready

Nutrition:

- Calories: 180 kcal Fat: 7 g Carbs: 6 g Protein: 12.8

14.Stuffed Mushrooms

Prep Time: 6 mins

Cook Time: 12 mins

Servings: 2

Ingredients:

- 2 teaspoons cumin powder

- 4 garlic cloves, peeled and minced

- 1 small onion, peeled and chopped

- 18 medium-sized white mushrooms

- Fine sea salt and freshly ground black pepper, to your liking

- A pinch ground allspice 2 tablespoons olive oil

Directions:

1. First, clean the mushrooms; remove the middle stalks from the mushrooms to prepare the "shells".

2. Grab a mixing dish and thoroughly combine the remaining items. Fill the mushrooms with the prepared mixture.

3. Cook the mushrooms at 345 degrees F heat for 12 minutes.

   Enjoy!

Nutrition:

- Calories: 179 kcal

- Fat: 14 g

- Carbs: 8.8 g

- Protein: 4.8

15. Crab Cakes

Prep Time: 20 mins

Cook Time: 10 mins

Servings: 2

Ingredients:

- ½ pound lump crabmeat, drained

- 2 tablespoons coconut flour

- 1 tablespoon mayonnaise

- ¼ teaspoon green Tabasco sauce

- 3 tablespoons butter

- 1 small egg, beaten

- ¾ tablespoon fresh parsley, chopped

- ½ teaspoon yellow mustard

- Salt and black pepper, to taste

Directions:

1. Mix together all the ingredients in a bowl except butter.

2. Make patties from this mixture and set aside.

3. Heat butter in a skillet over medium heat and add patties. Cook for about 10 minutes on each side and dish out to serve hot.

4. You can store the raw patties in the freezer for about 3 weeks for meal prepping.

5. Place patties in a container and place parchment paper in between the patties to avoid stickiness.

Nutrition:

*   Calories: 153 kcal

*   Fat: 10 g

*   Carbs: 6.8 g

16. Pesto Zucchini Noodles

Prep Time: 15 mins

Cook Time: 15 mins

Servings: 4

Ingredients:

- 4 zucchini, spiralized 1 tbsp avocado oil

- 2 garlic cloves, chopped 2/3 cup olive oil

- 1/3 cup parmesan cheese, grated , 2 cups fresh basil

- 1/3 cup almonds

- 1/8 tsp black pepper ¾ tsp sea salt

Directions:

1. Add zucchini noodles into a colander and sprinkle with ¼ teaspoon of salt. Cover and let sit for 30 minutes. Drain zucchini noodles well and pat dry.

2. Preheat the oven to 400 F. Place almonds on a parchment-lined baking sheet and bake for 6-8 minutes. Transfer toasted almonds into the food processor and process until coarse.

3. Add olive oil, cheese, basil, garlic, pepper, and remaining salt in a food processor with almonds and process until pesto texture.

4. Heat avocado oil in a large pan over medium-high heat.Add zucchini noodles and cook for 4-5 minutes.

5. Pour pesto over zucchini noodles, mix well and cook for 1 minute. Serve

Nutrition: Calories: 500 kcal; Fat: 44 g ; Carbs: 3 g ; Protein: 16 g

17.<u>Chicken Omelet</u>

Prep Time: 8 mins

Cook Time: 15mins **Servings**: 2

<u>*Ingredients*</u>:

- 4 bacon slices; cooked and crumbled

- 4 eggs   2 tablespoon homemade mayonnaise

- 2 tomato; chopped.

- 2-ounce rotisserie chicken; shredded

- 2 teaspoon mustard

- 2 small avocado; pitted, peeled and chopped.

- Salt and black pepper to the taste.

<u>*Directions*</u>:

1. In a bowl, mix eggs with some salt and pepper and whisk gently.

2. Heat up a pan over medium heat; spray with some cooking oil, add eggs and cook your omelet for 5 minutes

3. Add chicken, avocado, tomato, bacon, mayo and mustard on one half of the omelet.

4. Fold omelet, cover pan and cook for 5 minutes more

5. Transfer to a plate and serve

Nutrition:

- Calories: 380 kcal

- Fat: 30 g

- Carbs: 5 g

- Protein: 25 g

CHAPTER 3

SALAD RECIPES

18. <u>Greek Salad</u>

Prep Time: 5 mins

Cook Time: 0 mins

Servings: 1

<u>Ingredients</u>:

For Dressing:

- ½ teaspoon black pepper

- ¼ teaspoon salt

- ½ teaspoon oregano

- 1 tablespoon garlic powder

- 2 tablespoons Balsamic

- 1/3 cup olive oil

For Salad:

- ½ cup sliced black olives

- ½ cup chopped parsley, fresh

- 1 small red onion, thin-sliced

- 1 cup cherry tomatoes, sliced

- 1 bell pepper, yellow, chunked

- 1 cucumber, peeled, quarter and slice

- 4 cups chopped romaine lettuce

- ½ teaspoon salt

- 2 tablespoons olive oil

Directions:

1. In a small bowl, blend all of the ingredients for the dressing and

   let this set in the refrigerator while you make the salad.

2. To assemble the salad, mix together all the ingredients in a large-

   sized bowl and toss the veggies gently but thoroughly to mix.

   Serve

Nutrition:

- kcal: 234 g

- Carbohydrates: 48 g

- Protein: 5 g

19.Shrimp Cobb Salad

Prep Time: 25 mins

Cook Time: 10 mins

Servings: 2

Ingredients:

- 4 slices center-cut bacon

- 1 lb. large shrimp, peeled and deveined

- 1/2 teaspoon ground paprika

- 1/4 teaspoon ground black pepper

- 1/4 teaspoon salt, divided

- 2 1/2 tablespoons. Fresh lemon juice

- 1 1/2 tablespoons. Extra-virgin olive oil

- 1/2 teaspoon whole grain Dijon mustard

- 1 (10 oz.) package romaine lettuce hearts, chopped

- 2 cups cherry tomatoes, quartered

- 1 ripe avocado, cut into wedges

- 1 cup shredded carrots

Directions:

1. In a large skillet over medium heat, cook the bacon for 4 minutes on each side till crispy.

2. Take away from the skillet and place on paper towels; let cool for 5 minutes. Break the bacon into bits. Pour out most of the bacon fat, leaving behind only 1 tablespoon. in the skillet. Bring the skillet back to medium-high heat. Add black pepper and paprika to the shrimp for seasoning. Cook the shrimp around 2 minutes each side until it is opaque. Sprinkle with 1/8 teaspoon of salt for seasoning.

3. Combine the remaining 1/8 teaspoon of salt, mustard, olive oil and lemon juice together in a small bowl. Stir in the romaine hearts.

4. On each serving plate, place on 1 and 1/2 cups of romaine lettuce. Add on top the same amounts of avocado, carrots, tomatoes, shrimp and bacon.

Nutrition:

- Calories: 518 kcal

- Fat: 18.6 g

- Carbs: 22g

- Protein: 46.7g

20.<u>Mediterranean Salad</u>

Prep Time: 20 mins

Cook Time: 5 mins **Servings**: 1

<u>Ingredients</u>:

- 1 teaspoon balsamic vinegar

- 1/2 tablespoon basil pesto

- 1/2 cup lettuce

- 1/8 cup broccoli florets, chopped

- 1/8 cup zucchini, chopped

- 1/8 cup tomato, chopped

- 1/8 cup yellow bell pepper, chopped

- 1/2 tablespoons feta cheese, crumbled

<u>Directions</u>:

1. Arrange the lettuce on a serving platter.

2. Top with the broccoli, zucchini, tomato, and bell pepper.

3. In a bowl, mix the vinegar and pesto.

4. Drizzle the dressing on top.

5. Sprinkle the feta cheese and serve.

Nutrition:

- kcal: 101 g

- Carbohydrates: 7.2 g

- Protein: 4.2 g

- Fat: 6.1 g

21.Rice and Veggie Bowl

Prep Time: 5 mins

Cook Time: 15 mins

Servings: 1

Ingredients:

- 1/3 tbsp. coconut oil

- 1/2 tsp. ground cumin

- 1/2 tsp. ground turmeric

- 1/3 tsp. chili powder

- 1 red bell pepper, chopped

- 1/2 tbsp. tomato paste

- 1 bunch of broccolis, cut into bite-sized florets with short

  stems

- 1/2 tsp. salt, to taste

- 1 large red onion, sliced

- 1/2 garlic cloves, minced

- 1/2 head of cauliflower, sliced into bite-sized florets

- 1/2 cups cooked rice

- Newly ground black pepper to taste

Directions:

1. Start with warming up the coconut oil over medium-high heat.

2. Stir in the turmeric, cumin, chili powder, salt, and tomato paste.

3. Cook the content for 1 minute. Stir repeatedly until the spices are fragrant.

4. Add the garlic and onion. Fry for 2 to 3 minutes until the onions are softened.

5. Add the broccoli, cauliflower, and bell pepper. Cover then cook for 3 to 4 minutes and stir occasionally.

6. Add the cooked rice. Stir so it will combine well with the vegetables—Cook for 2 to 3 minutes. Stir until the rice is warm.

7. Check the seasoning and change to taste if desired.

8. Lessen the heat and cook on low for 2 to 3 more minutes so the flavors will meld.

9. Serve with freshly ground black pepper.

Nutrition:

- kcal: 262 g

- Carbohydrates: 37 g

- Protein: 9 g

- Fat: 9.1 g

22.Snap Pea Salad

Prep Time: 15 mins **Cook Time**: 3 mins **Servings**: 1

Ingredients:

- 1/2 tablespoons mayonnaise   3/4 teaspoon celery seed   1/4 cup cider vinegar   1/2 teaspoon yellow mustard   1/2 tablespoon sugar   Salt and pepper to taste   1 oz. radishes, sliced thinly   2 oz. sugar snap peas, sliced thinly

Directions:

1. In a bowl, combine the mayonnaise, celery seeds, vinegar, mustard, sugar, salt, and pepper.   Stir in the radishes and snap peas.   Refrigerate for 30 minutes.

Nutrition:

- kcal: 69 g Carbohydrates: 3.3 g Protein: 2.2 g Fat: 3.1 g

23.Parmesan Zucchini

Prep Time: 15 mins

Cook Time: 15 mins

Servings: 4

Ingredients:

- 4 zucchini, quartered lengthwise

- 2 tbsp fresh parsley, chopped

- 2 tbsp olive oil

- ¼ tsp garlic powder

- ½ tsp dried basil

- ½ tsp dried oregano

- ½ tsp dried thyme

- ½ cup parmesan cheese, grated

- Pepper

- Salt

Directions:

1. Preheat the oven to 350 F. Line baking sheet with parchment paper and set aside.

2. In a small bowl, mix together parmesan cheese, garlic powder, basil, oregano, thyme, pepper, and salt.

3. Arrange zucchini onto the prepared baking sheet and drizzle with oil and sprinkle with parmesan cheese mixture.

4. Bake in preheated oven for 15 minutes then broil for 2 minutes or until lightly golden brown.

5. Garnish with parsley and serve immediately.

Nutrition:

- kcal: 246 g Carbohydrates: 7.3 g Protein: 15 g

- Fat: 14 g

24.Tuscan Cauliflower Salad

Prep Time: 10 mins **Cook Time**: 10 mins**Servings**: 8

Ingredients:

- 4 cups Cauliflower florets 1 tablespoon Tuscan seasoning

- 1/4 cup Apple cider vinegar

Directions:

1. Add the Ingredients to a bowl and toss together.

2. Allow the mixture to settle for about 30 minutes. It can stay overnight. Serve. You can store it in your fridge for up to a week.

Nutrition:

- kcal: 116 g Carbohydrates: 4 g Protein: 5 g

- Fat: 9 g

25.<u>Coleslaw worth a Second Helping</u>

Prep Time: 20 mins

Cook Time: 10 mins

Servings: 6

<u>Ingredients</u>:

- 5 cups shredded cabbage

- 2 carrots, shredded

- 1/3 cup chopped fresh flat-leaf parsley

- ½ cup mayonnaise

- ½ cup sour cream

- 3 tablespoons apple cider vinegar

- 1 teaspoon kosher salt ½ teaspoon celery seed

<u>Directions</u>:

1. In a large bowl, combine the cabbage, carrots, and parsley.

2. In a small bowl, whisk the mayonnaise, sour cream, vinegar, salt, and celery seed until smooth. Pour the dressing over the vegetables and toss until coated. Transfer to a serving bowl and chill until ready to serve.

Nutrition:

- kcal: 182 g

- Carbohydrates: 7.1 g

- Protein: 2 g

- Fat: 16 g

CHAPTER 4

SNACKS AND APPETIZER RECIPES

26.Spicy Korean Cauliflower Bites

Prep Time: 5mins **Cook Time**: 25 mins **Servings**: 4

Ingredients:

CAULIFLOWER

- 1 large head cauliflower (large stalks removed, cut into bite-size "wings") 1 1/2 Tbsp avocado, sesame, or melted coconut oil (if avoiding oil, sub gochujang sauce)

SAUCE

- 1/2 cup Korean Gochujang Sauce (or store-bought – just ensure it's vegan/gluten-free)

- 1 Tbsp sesame oil or avocado oil (sub water if avoiding oil)

- 1/4 cup coconut aminos (or sub tamari, but reduce amount as it's saltier) 1 Tbsp maple syrup

- 1 pinch sea salt

- 1 Tbsp chili garlic sauce (for more heat // I like Huy Fong Foods brand) 2 Tbsp Water (to thin)

R SERVING (optional)

- Butter or romaine lettuce

- Whole garlic cloves, peeled (mincing optional)

- Fresh cilantro Sesame seeds Shredded carrots

Directions:

1. Preheat oven to 450 F (232 C) and line one large or two small baking sheets with parchment paper or a silicone baking sheet (like this one). Use more baking sheets as needed.

2. Add cauliflower to a large mixing bowl and toss with oil to coat. Then arrange on baking sheet(s) and roast for 10 minutes.

3. In the meantime, prepare sauce. To the same mixing bowl from earlier, add gochujang sauce, sesame oil (or water), coconut aminos, maple syrup, sea salt, and chili garlic sauce. Whisk to combine. Then taste and adjust flavor as needed. Add more chili garlic sauce for spice, coconut aminos for depth of flavor ("umami"), maple syrup for sweetness, or salt for saltiness.

4. Remove cauliflower from oven and increase heat to 500 degrees F (260 C). Add a few "wings" at a time to the sauce. Toss to coat generously, tap off excess, and then place back on baking sheet.

5. Coat all wings. Then return to oven and bake for 10-13 minutes more or until sizzling, golden brown on the edges, and tender (but not mushy).

6. While baking, prepare any additional serving elements, such as grated carrots, lettuce cups, or fresh garlic optional.

7. Serve immediately. Best when fresh. The wings can be refrigerated up to 3 days, or frozen (either at the glazed stage or the glazed and baked stage) up to 1 month and then reheated on the stovetop or in a 350-degree F (176 C) oven until warmed through.

Nutrition:

- Calories: 140 kcal

- Fat: 0.3 g

- Carbs: 30.4 g

- Protein: 6.0 g

27.Salmon Sandwich with Avocado and Egg

Prep Time: 15 mins

Cook Time: 10mins **Servings**: 4

Ingredients:

- 4 slices sourdough bread
- Olive oil 1 avocado
- Juice from one lime 2 eggs
- 4 ounces smoked salmon, sliced into strips (see note)
- Fresh ground pepper

Directions:

1. Brush both side of bread with olive oil, and either grill them on both sides or toast them until they are golden brown. Toasting them is easier, but grilling them gives them an out of this world grilled taste.

2. Mash avocado with a few squeezes of lime juice. Set aside.

3. Beat the eggs and then scramble them in a skillet over medium heat until they are just set.

4. Assemble sandwiches as follows: spread avocado over each slice of bread, top with eggs and a strip or two of salmon, and grind a little black pepper over all.

Nutrition:

- Calories: 435 kcal
- Fat: 12 g

- Carbs: 3.6 g

- Protein: 20.8

28. Wrapped Plums

Prep Time: 5 mins **Cook Time**: 0 mins **Servings**: 8

Ingredients:

- 2 ounces prosciutto, cut into 16 pieces

- 4 plums, quartered

- 1 tablespoon chives, chopped

- A pinch of red pepper flakes, crushed

Directions:

1. Wrap each plum quarter in a prosciutto slice, arrange them all on a platter, sprinkle the chives and pepper flakes all over and serve.

Nutrition:

- Calories: 20 kcal Fat: 1 g Carbs: 2 g Protein: 2g

29. Greek Style Mini Burger Pies

Prep Time: 10 mins **Cook Time**: 25 mins

Servings: 4

Ingredients:

- Sea salt ¼ cup garlic butter melt

- ¾ cup shredded mozzarella cheese

- ½ cup of parmesan cheese freshly grated

- 4 medium sized sweet potatoes

- 2 tsp freshly chopped parsley

Directions:

1. Heat the oven to 400 degrees Fahrenheit and brush the potatoes

with garlic butter and season each with pepper and salt. Arrange

the cut side down on a greased baking sheet until the flesh is

tender or they turn golden brown.

2. Remove them from the oven, flip the cut side up and top up with

parsley and parmesan cheese.

3. Change the settings of your instant fryer oven to broil and on

medium heat add the cheese and melt it. sprinkle salt and

pepper to taste. Serve them warm

Nutrition:

- Calories: 350 kcal

- Fat: 10 g

- Carbs: 10 g

- Protein: 10 g

30.Grilled Avocado Caprese Crostini

Prep Time: 10 mins **Cook Time**: 20 mins **Servings**: 2

Ingredients:

- 1 avocado thinly sliced

- 9 ounces ripened cherry tomatoes ounces fresh bocconcini in

  water 2 tsp balsamic glaze

- 8 pieces Italian baguette ½ a cup basil leaves

Directions:

1. Preheat your oven to 375 degrees Fahrenheit

2. Arrange your baking sheet properly before spraying them on top

  with olive oil. Bake your item of choice until they are well done

  or golden brown. Rub your crostini with the cut side of garlic

  while they are still warm and you can season them with pepper

  and salt.

3. Divide the basil leaves on each side of bread and top up with

tomato halves, avocado slices and bocconcini. Season it with

pepper and salt.

4. Broil it for 4 minutes and when the cheese starts to melt through

remove and drizzle balsamic glaze before serving.

Nutrition:

- Calories: 271 kcal

- Fat: 10 g

- Carbs: 38 g

- Protein: 10 g

31.Healthy 2 Ingredient Breakfast Cookies

Prep Time: 4 mins

Cook Time: 15 mins

Servings: 1

Ingredients:

- 1 ¾ cup of quick oats

- large ripe bananas

- 4 tsp peanut butter

- 1/3 cup crushed nuts of your choice

- ½ tsp pure vanilla extract

- ¼ cup shredded coconut

Directions:

1. Preheat your oven to 350 degrees Fahrenheit.

2. Mash the bananas in a bowl and add the oats and mix them well to combine. Fold any optional add ins such as ¼ cup chocolate chips. You can add honey to taste.

3. Line your baking tray with parchment paper and drop one tsp of cookie dough per cookie into your tray. Press down with a metal spoon into the shape of the cookies. Bake for 20 minutes depending on your oven or cook them until they are golden brown on top. Remove and allow to cool before serving.

Nutrition:

- Calories: 24 kcal

- Fat: 2 g

- Carbs: 6 g

- Protein: 4

32. Coconut Shrimp

Prep Time: 15 mins

Cook Time: 15 mins

Servings: 6

Ingredients:

- Salt and pepper

- 1-pound jumbo shrimp peeled and deveined

- ½ cup all-purpose flour

For batter:

- ½ cup beer

- 1 tsp baking powder

- ½ cup all-purpose flour

- 1 egg For coating:

- 1 cup panko bread crumbs

- 1 cup shredded coconut

Directions:

1. Line the baking tray with parchment paper.

2. In a shallow bowl add ½ cup flour for dredging and in another bowl whisk the batter ingredients. The batter should resemble a pancake consistency. If it is too thick add a little mineral or beer whisking in between. In another bowl mix together the shredded coconut and bread crumbs.

3. Dredge the shrimp in flour shaking off any excess before dipping in the batter and coat it with bread crumb mixture. Lightly press the coconut into the shrimp.

4. Place them into the baking sheet and repeat the process until you have several.

5. In a Dutch oven skillet heat vegetable oil until it is nice and hot fry the frozen shrimp batches for 3 minutes per side. Drain them on a paper towel lined plate.

6. Serve immediately with sweet chili sauce.

Nutrition:

- Calories: 400 kcal

- Fat: 11 g

- Carbs: 46 g

- Protein 30 g

33.<u>Sweet Peppers with Onions</u>

Prep Time: 9 mins

Cook Time: 5 mins

Servings: 2

<u>Ingredients</u>:

- 1 cup sliced green bell pepper
- 1 cup sliced red onion
- 1 tablespoon olive oil
- ½ teaspoon salt
- 1 tablespoon fresh lime juice

<u>Directions</u>:

1. Preheat an air fryer to 350 degrees F (175 degrees C). Combine green bell peppers, onion, olive oil, and salt in a large bowl. Transfer mixture to the air fryer basket.

2. Bake it for 7 to 9 minutes at 390 degrees F.

3. Transfer to a serving bowl. Drizzle the lime juice; toss to coat.

Serving Suggestion: Serve with pita bread

Variation Tip: Use oil spray instead of olive oil

<u>Nutrition</u>:

- Calories: 108 kcal
- Fat: 6 g
- Carbs: 8 g
- Protein: 1.7 g

34. Crispy Garlic Baked Potato Wedges

Prep Time: 5 mins

Cook Time: 10 mins

Servings: 3

Ingredients:

- 3 tsp salt

- 1 tsp minced garlic

- 6 large russet

- ¼ cup olive oil 1 tsp paprika

- 2/3 finely grated parmesan cheese

- 2 tsp freshly chopped parsley

Directions:

1. Preheat the oven into 350 degrees Fahrenheit and line the baking sheet with a parchment pepper.

2. Cut the potatoes into halfway length and cut each half in half lengthways again. Make 8 wedges.

3. In a small jug combine garlic, oil, paprika and salt and place your wedges in the baking sheets. Pour the oil mixture over the potatoes and toss them to ensure that they are evenly coated.

4. Arrange the potato wedges in a single layer on the baking tray and sprinkle salt and parmesan cheese if needed. Bake for 35 minutes turning the wedges once half side is cooked.

5. Flip the other side until they are both golden brown. Sprinkle parsley and the remaining parmesan before serving.

Nutrition:

- Calories: 324 kcal Fat: 6 g

- Carbs: 3 g

- Protein: 2g

CHAPTER 5

DINNER RECIPES

35. October Potato Soup

Prep Time: 8 mins

Cook Time: 20 mins

Servings: 3

Ingredients:

- 4 minced garlic cloves

- 2 teaspoon coconut oil

- 3 diced celery stalks

- 1 diced onion

- 2 teaspoon yellow mustard seeds

- 5 diced Yukon potatoes

- 6 cups vegetable broth

- 1 teaspoon oregano

- 1 teaspoon paprika

- 1/2 teaspoon cayenne pepper

- 1 teaspoon chili powder

- Salt and pepper to taste

Directions:

1. Begin by sautéing the garlic and the mustard seeds together in the oil in a large soup pot.

2. Next, add the onion and sauté the mixture for another five minutes.

3. Add the celery, the broth, the potatoes, and all the spices, and continue to stir.

4. Allow the soup to simmer for thirty minutes without a cover.

5. Next, Position about three cups of the soup in a blender, and

puree the soup until you've reached a smooth consistency. Pour

this back into the big soup pot, stir, and serve warm. 7

Nutrition: Calories 200; Carbs: 10g ;Fat: 6g; Protein: 7g

36.Red Quinoa and Black Bean Soup

Prep Time: 6 mins

Cook Time: 40 mins

Servings: 6

Ingredients:

- 1 1/4 cup red quinoa

- 4 minced garlic cloves

- 1/2 tablespoon coconut oil

- 1 diced jalapeno

- 3 cups diced onion

- 2 teaspoon cumin

- 1 chopped sweet potato

- 1 teaspoon coriander

- 1 teaspoon chili powder

- 5 cups vegetable broth

- 15 ounces black beans

- 1/2 teaspoon cayenne pepper

- 2 cups spinach

Directions:

1. Begin by bringing the quinoa into a saucepan to boil with two

   cups of water. Allow the quinoa to simmer for twenty minutes.

   Next, remove the quinoa from the heat.

2. To the side, heat the oil, the onion, and the garlic together in a

   large soup pot.

3. Add the jalapeno and the sweet potato and sauté for an

   additional seven minutes.

4. Next, add all the spices and the broth and bring the soup to a

   simmer for twenty-five minutes. The potatoes should be soft.

5. Prior to serving, add the quinoa, the black beans, and the spinach to the mix. Season, and serve warm.

Nutrition: Calories 208; Carbs: 20g ; Fat: 5g; Protein: 17g

37. Tilapia and Broccoli

Prep Time: 5 mins

Cook Time: 14 mins

Servings: 1

Ingredients:

- 6 oz. tilapia, frozen is fine

- 1 T butter

- 1 T garlic, minced or finely chopped

- 1 teaspoon of lemon pepper seasoning

- 1 cup broccoli florets, fresh or frozen, but fresh will be crisper

Directions:

1. Set the pre-warmed oven for 350 degrees.

2. Place the fish in an aluminum foil packet.

3. Arrange the broccoli around the fish to make an attractive

arrangement.

4. Sprinkle the lemon pepper on the fish.

5. Close the packet and seal, bake for 14 minutes.

6. Combine the garlic and butter. Set aside.

7. Remove the packet from the oven and transfer ingredients to a

plate.

8. Place the butter on the fish and broccoli.

Nutrition: Calories 360; Total Fat: 23g ; Protein: 27g; Carbs: 3.2g

38. Balsamic Beef and Mushrooms Mix

Preparation Time: 6 mins **Cook Time**: 8 mins **Servings:** 4

Ingredients:

- 2 pounds' beef, cut into strips ¼ cup balsamic vinegar 2 cups

  beef stock 1 tablespoon ginger, grated Juice of ½ lemon

- 1 cup brown mushrooms, sliced A pinch of salt and black

  pepper 1 teaspoon ground cinnamon

Directions:

1. Mix all the ingredients in your slow cooker, cover and cook on

   low for 8 hours. Divide everything between plates and serve.

Nutrition:

- Calories: 445 Fat: 13 Fiber 0.5Carbs 2.8

- Protein 70.6

39.Oregano Pork Mix

Preparation Time: 6 mins

Cook Time: 7h 6 minutes

Servings: 4

Ingredients:

- 2 pounds' pork roast

- 7 ounces' tomato paste

- 1 yellow onion, chopped

- 1 cup beef stock

- 2 tablespoons ground cumin

- 2 tablespoons olive oil

- 2 tablespoons fresh oregano, chopped

- 1 tablespoon garlic, minced

- ½ cup fresh thyme, chopped

Directions:

1. Heat up a sauté pan with the oil over medium-high heat, add the roast, brown it for 3 minutes on each side and then transfer to your slow cooker.

2. Add the rest of the ingredients, toss a bit, cover and cook on low for 7 hours.

3. Slice the roast, divide it between plates and serve.

Nutrition:

-   Calories: 620

-   Fat: 30

-   Fiber 6

-   Carbs 19

-   Protein 69

40. Chicken Breast Soup

Preparation Time: 6 min

Cooking Time: 4 hours

Servings: 4

Ingredients:

- 3 chicken breasts, skinless, boneless, cubed
- 2 celery stalks, chopped
- 2 carrots, chopped
- 2 tablespoons olive oil
- 1 red onion, chopped
- 3 garlic cloves, minced
- 4 cups chicken stock
- 1 tablespoon parsley, chopped

Directions:

1. In your slow cooker, mix all the ingredients except the parsley, cover and cook on High for 4 hours.

2. Add the parsley, stir, ladle the soup into bowls and serve.

Nutrition:

- Calories: 440
- Fat: 21

- Fiber 1.3

- Carbs 7.2

- Protein 54

41.Cauliflower Curry

Preparation Time: 6 minutes

Cook Time: 5 hours

Servings: 4

Ingredients:

- 1 cauliflower head, florets separated

- 2 carrots, sliced

- 1 red onion, chopped

- ¾ cup coconut milk

- 2 garlic cloves, minced

- 2 tablespoons curry powder

- A pinch of salt and black pepper

- 1 tablespoon red pepper flakes

- 1 teaspoon garam masala

Directions:

1. In your slow cooker, mix all the ingredients.

2. Cover, cook on high for 5 hours, divide into bowls and serve.

Nutrition:

- Calories: 155

- Fat: 11.2

- Fiber 5.3

- Carbs 14.4

- Protein 3.2

CHAPTER 6

DESSERT RECIPES

42. Peanut Butter Brownie

Prep Time: 15 mins

Cook Time: 1 mins

Servings: 2

Ingredients:

- 2 tablespoons peanut butter powder

- 2 tablespoons water

- 3 packets optavia double chocolate brownie fueling

- 1 cup of water

Directions:

1. Mix peanut butter powder with water and chocolate brownie in a bowl.

2. Divide this batter on a baking sheet lined with parchment paper into small mounds.

3. Cover and freeze for 40 minutes.

4. Serve.

Nutrition:

- Calories 180 Fat 5g

- Sodium 110mg

- Carbs 30g

- Fiber 5g

- Sugar 15g

- Protein 8g

43. Chocolate Cherry Cookie

Prep Time: 16 mins

Cook Time: 12 mins

Servings: 2

Ingredients:

- 1 Optavia dark chocolate covered cherry shake

- ½ teaspoons baking powder

- 2 tablespoons water

Directions:

1. At 350 degrees F, preheat your oven.

2. Mix cherry shake with water and baking powder in a bowl.

3. Divide this batter on a baking sheet, lined with parchment paper, into 8 small cookies.

4. Bake these cookies 12 minutes in the preheated oven.

5. Serve.

Nutrition:

- Calories 115

- Fat 20g

- Sodium 190mg

- Carbs 23.7g

- Fiber 0.9g

- Sugar 20g

- Protein 5g

44.Stuffed pears with almonds

Prep Time: 15 mins

Cook Time: 25 mins

Servings: 6

Ingredients:

- Spices

- 4 pinches cinnamon

- 3 ounces flour

- 3 ounces granulated sugar

- 2 tablespoons soup brown sugar

- 3 ounces almonds, powdered

- 1 ½ ounces frilled almond

- 1 ½ ounces hazelnut

- 3 ½ ounces butter

- 6 pears

Directions:

1. Mix butter with cinnamon, sugars, flour, almonds, hazelnut in a food processor.

2. Core the pears and divide the nuts mixture into these pears.

3. Place the stuffed pears on a baking sheet.

4. Bake these pears for 25 minutes in the oven at 300 degrees F.

5. Serve once cooled.

Nutrition:

- Calories 245 Fat 15g Sodium 95mg

- Carbs 38g

- Sugar 10g

- Protein 14g

45. Banana Bread

Prep Time: 6 mins

Cook Time: 40 mins

Servings: 6

Ingredients:

- ¾ cup sugar

- 1/3 cup butter

- 1 tbsp. vanilla extract

- 1 egg

- 2 bananas

- 1 tbsp. baking powder

- 1 and ½ cups flour

- ½ tbsp. baking soda

- 1/3 cup milk

- 1 and ½ tbsp. cream of tartar

- Cooking spray

Directions:

1. Mix in milk with cream of tartar, vanilla, egg, sugar, bananas and butter in a bowl and turn whole.

2. Mix in flour with baking soda and baking powder.

3. Blend the 2 mixtures, turn properly, move into oiled pan with cooking spray, put into air fryer and cook at 320°F for 40 minutes.

4. Remove bread, allow to cool, slice. Serve.

Nutrition:

- Calories: 540 Total Fat:16g Total carbs: 28g

46.Mini Lava Cakes

Prep Time: 6 mins

Cook Time: 20 mins

Servings: 3

Ingredients:

- 1 egg

- 4 tbsp. sugar

- 2 tbsp. olive oil

- 4 tbsp. milk

- 4 tbsp. flour

- 1 tbsp. cocoa powder

- ½ tbsp. baking powder

- ½ tbsp. orange zest

Directions:

1. Mix in egg with sugar, flour, salt, oil, milk, orange zest, baking powder and cocoa powder, turn properly. Move it to oiled ramekins.

2. Put ramekins in air fryer and cook at 320°F for 20 minutes.

3. Serve warm.

Nutrition:

- Calories: 325

- Total Fat: 8.2g

- Total carbs: 12g

47.<u>Crispy Apples</u>

Prep Time: 12 mins

Cook Time: 10 mins

Servings: 4

Ingredients:

- 2 tbsp. cinnamon powder

- 5 apples

- ½ tbsp. nutmeg powder

- 1 tbsp. maple syrup

- ½ cup water

- 4 tbsp. butter

- ¼ cup flour

- ¾ cup oats

- ¼ cup brown sugar

Directions:

1. Get the apples in a pan, put in nutmeg, maple syrup, cinnamon and water.

2. Mix in butter with flour, sugar, salt and oat, turn, put spoonful of blend over apples, get into air fryer and cook at 350°F for 10 minutes.

3. Serve while warm.

Nutrition:

- Calories: 385

- Total Fat: 5.5g

- Total carbs: 12.2g

48. Ginger Cheesecake

Prep Time: 22 mins

Cook Time: 20 mins

Servings: 6

Ingredients:

- 2 tbsp. butter

- ½ cup ginger cookies

- 16 oz. cream cheese

- 2 eggs

- ½ cup sugar 1 tbsp. rum

- ½ tbsp. vanilla extract ½ tbsp. nutmeg

Directions:

1. Spread pan with the butter and sprinkle cookie crumbs on

   the bottom.

2. Whisk cream cheese with rum, vanilla, nutmeg and eggs, beat properly and sprinkle the cookie crumbs.

3. Put in air fryer and cook at 340° F for 20 minutes.

4. Allow cheese cake to cool in fridge for 2 hours before slicing. Serve.

Nutrition:

- Calories: 310

- Total Fat: 9.6g

- Total carbs: 16g

49. Blueberries Stew

Preparation Time: 12 mins **Cook Time**: 10 mins **Servings:** 4

Ingredients:

- 2 cups blueberries 3 tablespoons stevia 1 and ½ cups pure apple juice   1 teaspoon vanilla extract

Directions:

1. In a pan, combine the blueberries with stevia and the other ingredients, bring to a simmer and cook over medium-low heat for 10 minutes.   Divide into cups and serve cold.

Nutrition:

- Calories: 190

- Fat: 5.2 Fiber 3.2

- Carbs 9.3

- Protein 4.3

50. Cherry Compote

Preparation Time: 2 hours

Cooking Time: 0 minutes

Servings: 6

Ingredients:

- 2 peaches, pitted, halved

- 1 cup cherries, pitted

- ½ cup grape juice

- ½ cup strawberries

- 1 tablespoon liquid honey

- 1 teaspoon vanilla extract

- 1 teaspoon ground cinnamon

Directions:

1. Pour grape juice in the saucepan.

2. Add vanilla extract and ground cinnamon. Bring the liquid to boil.

3. After this, put peaches, cherries, and strawberries in the hot grape juice and bring to boil.

4. Remove the mixture from heat, add liquid honey, and close the lid.

5. Let the compote rest for 20 minutes.

Nutrition:

- Calories 78

- Fat 0.3 g

- Fiber 2.3 g

- Carbs 19.7 g

- Protein 0.7 g

Conclusion

With regards to food, I have learned to see food as the major source of energy that powers my body and to find profound fulfillment in eating things that are nutritious. The Lean and Green diet cookbook is a healthy and tasty approach to eating healthy and losing weight while also enjoying your favorite foods. There is no reward better than the satisfaction you derive from making the right choices. Kick out the old emotional eating habits of using food as a reward and embrace a new healthier eating habit with this Lean and Green diet cookbook.

CPSIA information can be obtained
at www.ICGtesting.com
Printed in the USA
BVHW092257210621
610124BV00009B/1756